HOW THINGS WORK!

SENSORS

ADE DEANE-PRATT

WAYLAND

First published in 2011 by Wayland

Copyright © Wayland 2011

Wayland
338 Euston Road
London NW1 3BH

Wayland Australia
Level 17/207 Kent Street
Sydney NSW 2000

Editor: Julia Adams

Produced by Tall Tree Ltd
Editors, Tall Tree: Rob Colson, Jennifer Sanderson
Consultant: Penny Johnson
Step-by-step photography: Ed Simkins, Caroline Watson
Designer: Jonathan Vipond

British Library Cataloguing in Publication Data
 Deane-Pratt, Ade.
  Sensors. -- (How things work)
  1. Detectors--Juvenile literature.
  I. Title II. Series
  681.2-dc22

  ISBN-13: 9780750261241

Printed in China

Wayland is a division of Hachette Children's Books,
an Hachette UK company.
www.hachette.co.uk

Picture credits

The publisher would like to thank the following for their kind permission to reproduce their photographs:
key: (t) top; (c) centre; (b) bottom; (l) left; (r) right
1 and 21 (tr) Deborah Cheramie/iStock; 2 and 7 (c) Grafissimo/iStock; 4 Tobkatrina/Dreamstime.com; 5 Suljo/Dreamstime.com; 7 (tr) Ali Rıza Yıldız/ Dreamstime.com; 8 Enruta/Dreamstime.com; (tl) Alshadsky/Dreamstime.com, (cr) ilbusca/iStock, (bl) Goldenkb/ Dreamstime.com; 11 (tl) Kaczor58/ Dreamstime.com, (tr) US Navy, (br) Wenhai Tang/ Dreamstime.com; 12 Aprescindere/Dreamstime.com; 13 (t) Valeriy Kirsanov/ Dreamstime.com, (b) Marc Slingerland/Dreamstime.com; 14 Oriontrail/ Dreamstime.com; 15 and 32 Mark Goddard/iStock, (c) JulienGrondin/iStock, (br) Vladimir Mucibabic/ Dreamstime.com; 17 (tl) Bennewitz/iStock, (tr) Susan Quinland-stringer/Dreamstime.com, (br) woraput/ iStock; 19 (tr) Dbvirago/Dreamstime.com, (bl) Photosoup/Dreamstime.com, (br) Papa1266/ Dreamstime.com; 20 Dreamstime; 21 (tl) James Steidl/ Dreamstime.com, (b) Mark Kostich/iStock

Disclaimer

CONTENTS

WHAT ARE SENSORS?

Sensors detect things in the world around us, such as sound, light, smell, temperature and pressure. We have natural sensors in our bodies, and we also use artificial sensors.

WHAT DO SENSORS DETECT?

Natural and artificial sensors detect a lot of the same things. For example, eyes and cameras both detect light, while ears and microphones detect sound. Some sensors are designed to detect things we cannot sense ourselves. For example, we keep ourselves safe using sensors that detect dangerous chemicals that we cannot smell, such as carbon monoxide. Other sensors may detect kinds of light that we cannot see. A television remote control sends invisible signals to the television, where a special sensor detects them.

Cameras contain a type of light sensor that can record images.

4

ARTIFICIAL SENSORS

Most artificial sensors are used as part of more complicated machines, for example in a greenhouse's central heating system. Here the sensors activate part of a machine when they detect certain conditions.

This book looks at both natural and artificial sensors. The project pages will show you how to make your own sensors, including a sound sensor and a barometer.

Many of the vegetables we eat are grown in huge greenhouses. Sensors detect the temperature. Heaters are switched on when it gets too cold, and automatic windows are opened if it gets too hot.

LIGHT SENSORS

We use light sensors to detect the colour and brightness of light. Cameras capture images by focusing light onto a light sensor using a lens, in a similar way to our eyes.

HOW DOES IT WORK?

Light enters a camera through the lens and hits a sensor at the back. In a digital camera, the sensor converts the pattern of light into electrical signals, which are recorded as an image.

Eyes work in a similar way to cameras. Light enters our eyes through the pupil. It travels through a lens and then hits the area at the back of the eye called the retina, which is the light sensor. The image on the retina is inverted or upside down. The retina sends signals to our brain where the image is converted to the one we see.

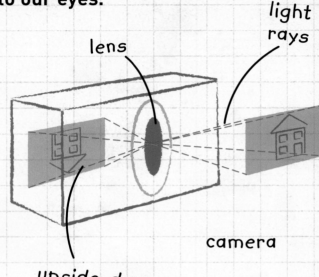

lens

light rays

upside-down image on a light-sensor

camera

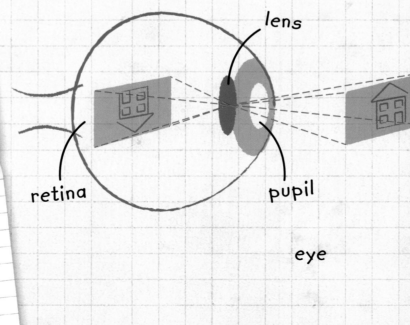

lens

retina

pupil

eye

Try it !

The size of your pupil changes depending on how bright the light is. Stand in a well-lit room in front of a mirror. Close your eyes for 30 seconds. Now open your eyes and look in the mirror. What happens to the size of your pupils?

LIGHT SENSORS IN ACTION

Cameras may capture a single image by recording the pattern of light at one moment, or record moving images by sensing changes in the light over time. Simple light sensors that detect only the level of light may be included inside other machines, such as street lights.

Street lights are set to turn on automatically at dusk when it starts to get dark and turn off at dawn when it gets light. They use sensors to detect the change in the light.

TV cameras record changes in the pattern and brightness of light to produce a moving image.

If the lenses in our eyes are unable to focus the light on the retina, we will not see things very clearly. Glasses act as an additional lens to help focus the light.

SENSING INVISIBLE LIGHT

Artificial sensors can detect forms of light, such as X-rays, radio waves and infrared, that we cannot see with our eyes.

HOW DOES IT WORK?

Doctors and dentists use X-rays to photograph what is underneath our skin. X-ray machines send invisible X-rays through our bodies. The X-rays pass through skin and flesh, but not through bones. A sensor detects the rays that pass right through the body to produce an image of the bones.

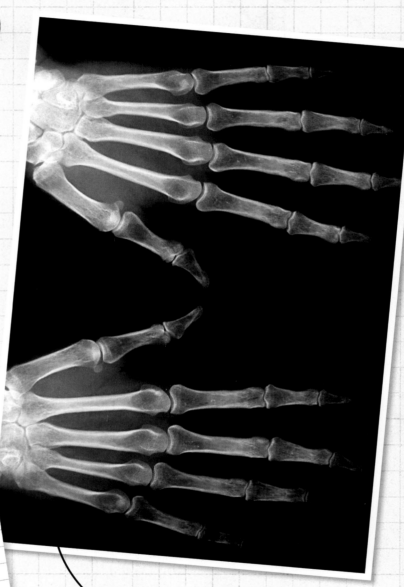

This X-ray of a person's hands allows doctors to see all the bones clearly. The doctor could easily see if any bones are broken

Try it !

Most cameras can detect infrared light. Point a television remote control at the lens of a digital camera. Press one of the buttons on the remote. Can you see the end of the remote light up in the image on the camera's screen?

Television remote controls send out infrared light in pulses. The pulses are detected by a sensor in the television. A computer inside the television turns the pulses into a code that tells it what action to take.

SENSING INVISIBLE LIGHT IN ACTION

We can use invisible light sensors to make cameras that see through solid objects, or to open doors automatically. Infrared is used in remote controls to operate televisions and DVD players.

sensor

Automatic doors have sensors that detect a small beam of invisible microwaves. Moving near the door breaks the beam and tells the door to open.

The remote controls for some computer games give off invisible radio waves. These waves pass through objects such as our bodies, so that we do not block the signal as we move around.

9

SENSORS IN SPACE

Artificial satellites orbiting Earth use sensors to detect radio waves and telephone signals. This makes it possible to relay long-distance telephone calls and broadcast television programmes around the world.

HOW DO THEY WORK?

When the number for a long-distance call is dialled from a mobile phone, the signal is transmitted to a local antenna, which then relays it to a satellite ground station. The ground station beams the signal to a satellite orbiting Earth. The satellite transmits the signal to another satellite on the network, which beams it down to a ground station. The call is routed to the receiver's local antenna cell by the phone network. The signals are detected by the receiver's phone and it rings.

Try it !

Hold a torch out in front of you close to a wall and turn it on. Now start to step backwards slowly, keeping the torch facing the wall. As you move further away from the wall, the area lit up on the wall gets bigger. In the same way, the further a satellite is from Earth, the larger the area it can see.

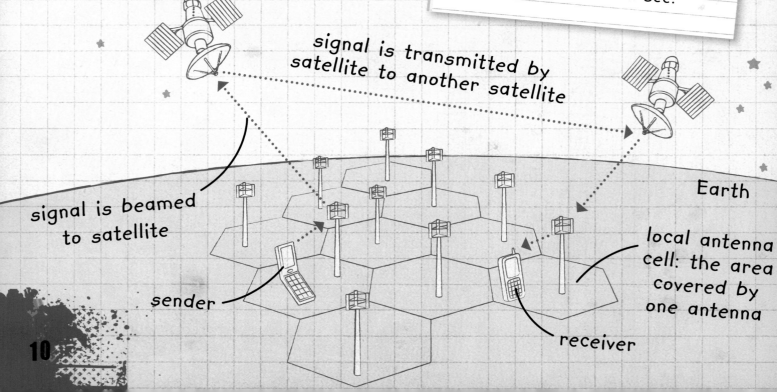

signal is transmitted by satellite to another satellite

signal is beamed to satellite

Earth

local antenna cell: the area covered by one antenna

sender

receiver

Satnav machines use a system of satellites, called the Global Positioning System (GPS), to work out where people are. A GPS receiver finds the satellites, works out the distance to each one and uses this information to work out its own location. The more satellites the receiver finds, the more accurate the results.

Satellite telephones send radio waves to a satellite in orbit. This satellite receives the message and sends it back to a receiver at the surface. Satellite phones do not need ground stations, so they are used by reporters working in remote locations.

SATELLITES IN ACTION

We use satellites for different forms of communication, such as satellite telephones and broadcasting. We can also use satellites to find out exactly where we are on Earth's surface, using a system called GPS.

Satellite TV is a system in which a broadcast centre sends a programme signal to a satellite above Earth. The satellite sends the signal back down to Earth where it is picked up by a satellite dish on a house.

SEEING WITH SOUND

Sounds are vibrations that travel through the air and through other materials. It is possible to create an image of the world around us by bouncing sounds off objects and recording the echoes they send back.

HOW DOES IT WORK?

Ultrasound is sound that is too high-pitched for humans to hear. Doctors use ultrasound to examine organs in the body and to look at unborn babies in the womb. As sound passes through the body, it produces echoes. The ultrasound machine emits sound and detects the returning echoes when it is placed on or over the body part being studied. The echoes are analysed by a computer in the ultrasound machine and transformed into moving pictures.

This image of a baby in its mother's womb was made using ultrasound

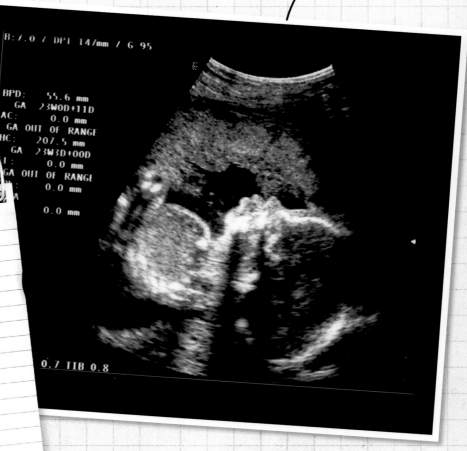

B: 7.0 / DPI 14/mm / G 95

BPD: 55.6 mm
  GA   23W0D+11D
AC: 0.0 mm
  GA OUT OF RANGE
HC: 207.5 mm
  GA   23W3D+00D
          0.0 mm
  GA OUT OF RANGE
          0.0 mm

          0.0 mm

0.7 TIB 0.8

Try it !

Find a large room, such as a sports hall, and shout 'hello' as loudly as you can. What do you hear?

large ears —— pick up the faint echoes

Bats detect insects flying nearby by listening to the echoes of their high-pitched calls. The bat can work out how far away the insect is and even how fast it is flying.

SOUND SENSORS IN ACTION

Various systems of echoes can be used to create images. For example, sonar is used by marine biologists to study plant and animal life in the oceans.

Submarines can use sonar to detect ships and other submarines underwater. Sound waves are reflected off objects in the submarine's path, creating echoes that bounce back to the vessel and are picked up by the sonar equipment.

VIBRATING SOLIDS

We use artificial sensors to detect vibrations that we cannot feel ourselves. Animals and plants use natural sensors to detect vibrations made by prey.

HOW DOES IT WORK?

Seismometers are special sensors that detect vibrations in the ground. They are used to predict and measure the strength of earthquakes. Seismometers consist of an electromagnet within a case. During an earthquake, the electromagnet keeps still while the case moves or vibrates with the ground's shaking. The vibrations are shown as squiggly lines on a computer screen. The height of the lines shows how big the vibrations are and the strength of the earthquake.

The number of lines on this readout from a seismometer shows how often the vibrations from an earthquake have passed through a particular place

Try it !

Press your ear onto a table and give the table a gentle tap. You will hear the tap quite loudly as the vibrations are passing through the table to your ear.

VIBRATING SOLIDS IN ACTION

Venus fly traps and spiders have natural sensors. The sensors in a spider's legs detect vibrations in the spider's web made by struggling insects caught by it. Artificial sensors that detect vibrations are used in car alarms.

Venus fly traps are plants that feed on insects. Some of their leaves form a cup. Special hairs on the surface of these leaves vibrate as an insect moves over them, causing the leaves to snap shut and trap the insect.

The sensor in a car alarm detects vibrations that could be caused by someone attempting to break into the vehicle. When vibrations are felt, the sensors trigger the alarm and a siren sounds.

Liquid rock, called magma, moves underneath a volcano, causing vibrations in the ground that a sensor can detect. The vibrations become stronger days before the volcano erupts, so the sensor can act as an early warning system.

FEELING THE HEAT

We have sensors in our skin that tell us how hot or cold it is. We make artificial sensors to detect changes in temperature or to measure exactly what the temperature is.

HOW DOES IT WORK?

Some thermometers sense temperature using liquid inside a thin tube. When the temperature rises, the liquid in the thermometer heats up. As the liquid gets warmer, it expands to fill a bigger space. When the temperature cools, so does the liquid, and it contracts into a smaller space again. As the liquid expands and contracts, it moves up and down the tube, showing the temperature.

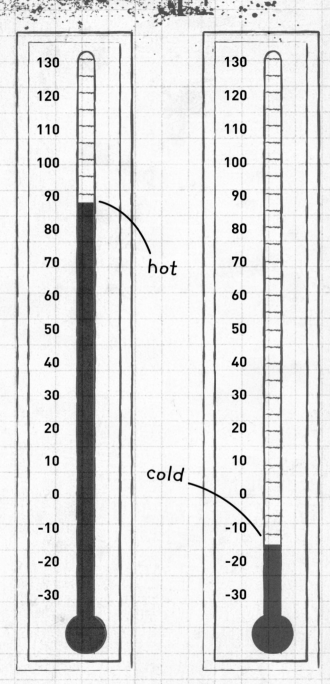

hot

cold

Try it !

Use a thermometer to record your own temperature by placing it gently under your armpit for about a minute. Compare the temperature of your body with room temperature. Then place the thermometer inside the fridge for 30 minutes, and see what the temperature is.

The scale on a thermometer tells you what the temperature is when the liquid reaches a particular height. The liquid rises as the temperature increases.

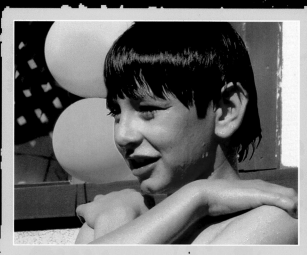

Sensors inside an oven make sure that the temperature stays at the level we have chosen on the dial.

Temperature sensors in our skin tell us how warm the air is around us. When it gets too cold our skin breaks out in goosebumps.

TEMPERATURE SENSORS IN ACTION

Our bodies and many machines will only work properly at certain temperatures. We use sensors to make sure they stay at or near the right temperature. Sensors can also be used to detect the approach of warm objects, such as someone's body.

Our bodies give off a lot of heat. Some burglar alarms use sensors to detect body heat. They are set off by the approach of a person or an animal, such as a cat.

UNDER PRESSURE

Pressure is the force on a particular area. We use sensors to measure pressure. This can help us to check that bicycle tyres have been inflated correctly, how much we weigh and what the weather will be like.

HOW DOES IT WORK?

Pressure is produced when one object pushes against another. Sensors can measure the pressure of gases, such as air. A barometer is a pressure sensor that is used to work out weather conditions. It senses how high or low the air pressure is around it. When the pressure is low, this means that damp air is rising to form clouds, which cause rain. High pressure usually means a dry, sunny day.

A mercury barometer uses the liquid metal mercury to measure atmospheric pressure. When the atmospheric pressure is high, the mercury rises.

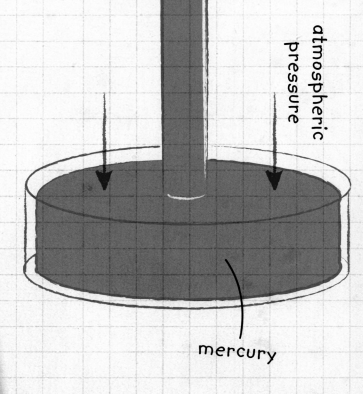

vacuum

weight of mercury presses back against atmospheric pressure

atmospheric pressure

mercury

Try it !

Blow up a balloon until you cannot get any more air into it. Let out a little air. How strong was the airflow of the air escaping? Now do the same, but this time, blow up the balloon until it is only about half full.

Air pressure decreases as aeroplanes climb in the atmosphere. Inside a cockpit, the pressure sensors tell the pilot how high the aeroplane is flying.

PRESSURE SENSORS IN ACTION

Not only do pressure sensors measure the pressure of gases, such as the air, but they can also measure the pressure of liquids, such as the blood in our bodies. Divers carry pressure sensors with them. The deeper they dive, the greater the pressure of the water around them. They use the pressure sensor to work out how deep they are.

Cyclists and motorists use gauge pressure sensors to make sure that their tyres are correctly inflated. The sensors compare the pressure of the air inside the tyre to the pressure of the air outside it.

Pressure sensors measure the pressure of the blood going around your body. Doctors measure blood pressure to check that it is at a healthy level.

MAGNETIC SENSORS

Some sensors can detect magnetic fields. We can use magnetic sensors to search people for weapons or to search the ground for treasure.

The magnetic field from a bar magnet moves tiny iron filings scattered around it into a distinctive pattern. The pattern shows the shape of the magnetic field

HOW DOES IT WORK?

Magnets can affect materials made of certain metals, such as iron or steel. The area around a magnet where it can affect a metal is called its magnetic field. Magnetic fields are also formed when an electric current flows. A metal detector produces a magnetic field when electricity passes through it. Metal objects nearby can affect this magnetic field. The detector senses the changes in the magnetic field caused by the metal. It makes a beep to show there is something metallic close by.

Try it !

Take a magnet and hold it close to several different objects. Which materials are attracted to the magnet? Try a metal spoon and then a plastic spoon. Does the magnet attract plastic or wood?

Before boarding an aeroplane, passengers pass through a security gate. The gate contains a magnetic sensor that makes a beep if the person is carrying any metal objects.

MAGNETIC SENSORS IN ACTION

Magnetic sensors are used to ensure passenger safety at airports and train stations. They are also used for medical purposes in the form of MRI scans.

Metal detectors can be used to hunt for metallic treasure buried in the ground.

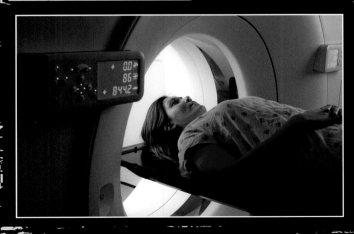

Magnetic Resonance Imaging (MRI) is a way to obtain a detailed image of the inside of our bodies. First, a magnetic field is set up in the body, then a sensor detects the pattern of magnetism and uses it to make the image.

Make a sound sensor

This sensor will take invisible vibrations and turn them into visible ripples in water.

what you need

- two A4-sized pieces of card
- scissors
- foil tray
- cling film
- bowl of water
- bendy drinking straw
- table tennis ball
- sticky tape

cut here

1 Fold both pieces of card in half. Hold the tray against the folded ends and mark the tray's depth on each piece of card. Cut out the rectangles from each piece of card. These will be the base for your sensor.

2 Cut a square 10 cm x 10 cm (4 in x 4 in) in the middle of the tray. Stretch cling film over the top of the tray to seal it.

10 cm (4 in)

3 Stand the card on its side to make a holder for the foil tray. Rest the foil tray in the card so that the hole is at the back and clingfilm is at the front. Put the bowl of water in front of the tray.

4 Make four cuts in each end of the straw so that they split open. Spread out the ends into a cross shape.

5 Tape one end of the straw to the table tennis ball.

6 Carefully tape the other end of the straw to the cling film so that the table tennis ball rests on the surface of the water. Speak into one side of the tray through the hole, and watch as your voice moves the ball and creates ripples in the bowl of water.

Take it further

- Test your sound sensor with different sounds and see what ripples they produce.
- Is there a difference between the ripples of high and low notes?

Make a pinhole camera

The very first cameras looked similar to this pinhole camera.

what you need

- small cardboard box
- scissors
- glue
- cup
- paint and paintbrush
- tracing paper
- sticky tape
- kitchen foil
- needle
- towel

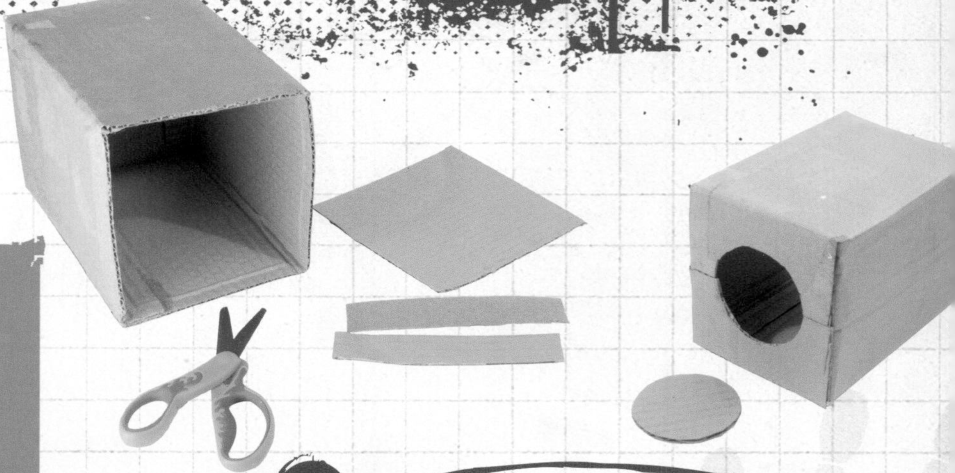

1 Cut the flaps from one end of the cardboard box. Glue down the flaps at the other end. Use the cup to draw a circle on the closed end, and cut it out.

2 Paint the inside of the box with the black paint. This will make the image clearer. You can decorate the outside, too.

3 Measure a square of tracing paper, just a little larger than the end of the box, and tape it tightly over the open end.

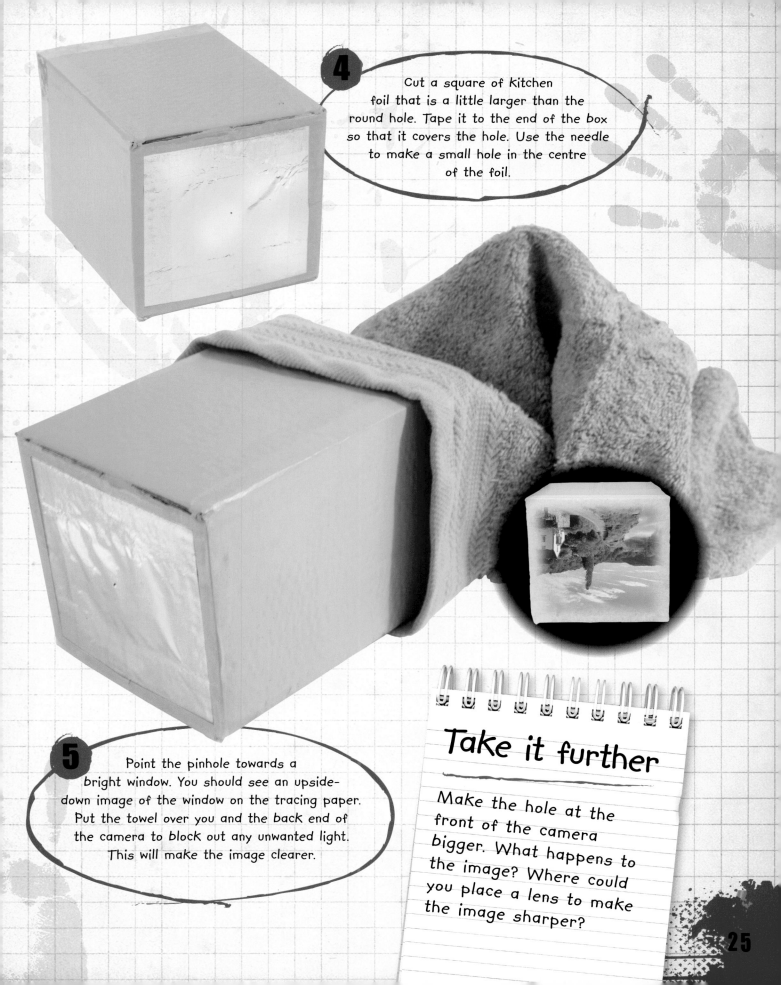

4 Cut a square of kitchen foil that is a little larger than the round hole. Tape it to the end of the box so that it covers the hole. Use the needle to make a small hole in the centre of the foil.

5 Point the pinhole towards a bright window. You should see an upside-down image of the window on the tracing paper. Put the towel over you and the back end of the camera to block out any unwanted light. This will make the image clearer.

Take it further

Make the hole at the front of the camera bigger. What happens to the image? Where could you place a lens to make the image sharper?

Make a barometer

Use your barometer to see if you can predict the weather.

what you need

- scissors
- balloon
- elastic band
- glass jar
- felt-tip pens
- toothpick
- straw
- sticky tape
- cardboard box

1 Cut the neck off the balloon. Stretch the rest of the balloon over the top of the jar. Fasten it in place with the elastic band.

balloon

elastic band

2 Using a felt-tip pen, colour the pointed end of the toothpick. Tape the toothpick to one end of the straw with the pointed end pointing outwards.

sticky tape

3 Tape the other end of the straw to the balloon that is stretched over the jar.

4 Cut one side out of the cardboard box and place the jar in the box with the pointer pointing sideways. Draw arrows on the card behind the pointer. One arrow should point up, the other down.

5 Note how the pointer moves each day as the weather changes. Record the position of the barometer each day and note the weather, whether it is cloudy or sunny, warm or cold.

Take it further

Can you see a pattern in the recordings? Which places on the chart are most likely to mean dry weather? Replace the arrows with weather symbols and see if you can forecast the weather.

Make a thermometer

Tell the temperature with this easy-to-make thermometer.

what you need

- measuring jug
- water
- surgical spirit
- 500 ml (1 pint) narrow-necked plastic bottle with lid
- blue food colouring
- clear drinking straw
- modelling clay
- marker pen

1 Using the measuring jug, measure out 60 ml (2 fl oz) of water and an equal amount of surgical spirit. Pour them into the bottle and add a few drops of food colouring. Put the lid onto the bottle and shake it gently to mix in the colouring.

2 Wrap some modelling clay around the middle of the straw. Push the straw into the bottle so that the modelling clay seals the neck of the bottle. Push the straw through the modelling clay so that the end of the straw is just above the bottom of the bottle.

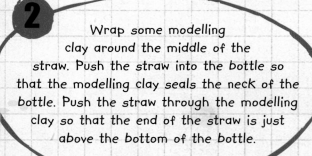

3 Test the thermometer by warming the bottle with your hands, and see the mixture rise up through the straw.

4 Measure different temperatures by placing the thermometer in direct sunlight or in a cool room. Also try placing it in a bowl of warm water or a bowl of cold water. How does the level of liquid in the straw change as the temperature changes?

Take it further

Measure the temperature of various places with your thermometer and another one with a scale on it. You can then mark a scale on your thermometer showing which temperature is represented by each different level of liquid.

GLOSSARY

artificial
Made by humans. A camera is an artificial light sensor, while the eye is a natural light sensor.

barometer
An instrument that measures atmospheric pressure. It is used to predict the weather.

carbon monoxide
A colourless gas with no smell, which is highly poisonous.

electromagnet
A device made of a coil of insulated wire wrapped around an iron core, which becomes magnetised when an electric current flows through the wire.

microwave
An electromagnetic wave of extremely high frequency and a short wavelength. Microwaves are used in mobile telephones and to cook food.

MRI (Magnetic Resonance Imaging)
The use of magnetism to produce images of objects. Doctors use MRI to detect problems in patients.

pitch
How high or low a sound is.

pupil
The dark part of the eye that changes size in response to the brightness of light.

radio wave
An electromagnetic wave that has a low frequency and a long wavelength. Radio waves are invisible to the human eye.

retina
The layer of light sensors at the back of the eye. The retina sends signals to our brain where the image is converted to the one we see.

satellite
An object that orbits around the Earth or another planet. Artificial satellites are used for communications and weather information.

satellite phone
A type of telephone that sends signals straight to a satellite rather than via a local antenna and ground station. This means that it can be used in remote parts of the world.

satnav
A navigational system that uses satellites to work out where an object is.

orbit
The path of a satellite, such as the Moon, as it moves around another body, such as Earth. Satellites are held in orbit by the force of gravity.

sonar
A system for the detection of objects by emitting sound pulses and detecting, or measuring, their return. Submarines use sonar to find other submarines.

thermal
Relating to heat.

ultrasound
The medical use of high-pitched sound waves, especially to produce images of the inside of the body or of a developing foetus in the womb.

X-ray
A form of electromagnetic radiation that has a very high frequency. X-rays can penetrate some solids and are used in medicine produce images of the body.

TOPIC WEB

Use this topic web to discover themes and ideas in subjects that are related to how sensors work.

History
Metal detectors play an important role in finding land mines in war zones. What sensors have been used in times of war in the past? Draw a spider diagram to represent your findings.

English
Metal detectors have been used to find treasure from the ancient world. Use the Internet to find articles about these discoveries. Imagine you are the treasure hunter. Write a journal entry explaining what you found and how you felt when you found it.

Design and Technology
Use sensors to make an alarm that will protect either someone or something. Use a design sheet to plan your alarm and then build a prototype of your alarm. What materials have you used?

Sensors

Geography
A seismometer is used to measure earthquakes. Draw a detailed diagram to explain what happens during an earthquake. Using the Internet to find out about recent earthquakes, write a report on one of them. Think about the impact the earthquake had on the local people and supplies. What did rescue services do to help these people?

Science
Build your own doorbell using simple parts, such as switches, batteries and buzzers. Draw a circuit diagram to illustrate what you have built.

INDEX

HOW THINGS WORK!
Contents of all titles in the series:

WAYLAND